For Martí, Carla and Berta, because you fly very high and make your dreams come true.

Anna Obiols & Subi

In cooperation with Fundació Gala - Salvador Dalí

1st edition: May 2023

Laureà Miró, 375 (Nau 2)
08980 Sant Feliu de Llobregat (Barcelona)
Tel.: 93 218 34 58
editorial@editorialmediterrania.com
www.editorialmediterrania.com

ISBN: 978-84-19028-54-9
LD: B 4111-2023
Original design: Endoradisseny
Print: Grupo Ormo

Little Dalí

Anna Obiols

Illustrations by Subi

Editorial Mediterrània

Once upon a time, there was a child named Salvador, but everyone called him Salvi. One of his favorite pastimes was to run barefoot on the beach while he tried to catch his hoop.

One afternoon, while he was playing, he noticed that there was something in the water, near the sand. He got closer, and saw that the waves had swept along a key. He did not think twice, and picked it up.

Enthralled by the mystery that could lie behind that key, he jumped on his elephant, and let his imagination lead the way.

Along the way, Salvi came across a very special cook. He made clocks out of eggs as if they were omelettes. Each one was made to strike at a specific hour. The clock set for that time then struck three o'clock; very strange things were happening then in that corner of the desert. Very intrigued, he asked the cook, 'Good morning, cook from the desert, do you know by any chance what this key opens?'
'Let's see...,' he said.

Salvi brought the key closer to
him so that he could see it better.
'Oooh! This is a magic key. Look, if you
want my advice, leave your elephant and
get on this boat. She knows the way, and she
will guide you.'
Little Salvi did not really understand what was happening,
but he was so curious about the key that he did as the cook
said, and he got on the boat, which started to take flight.

When he was closer to the sky than he was to the ground, he
noticed that the clouds were shaped like objects and characters,
and he tried to guess what or who they were.

He arrived at a very high tower that was topped by several giant eggs. He got off the boat, and climbed some spiral stairs that led to a very unusual entrance.

Blinded by the outer light, Salvi found the inside of the tower very dark and mysterious. He immediately saw that there were doors and drawers everywhere. Very excited, he started to open them. After a while, he became discouraged because he saw that the key did not fit in any of the locks that he had tried to open, and he felt sad.

Before leaving, he tried opening, very discouraged, the last drawers that were left. When he did not expect anything anymore, Salvi saw how the key fit, turned and opened the last drawer. What a surprise! Would there be a treasure? A chest? A map hiding a secret? Or maybe...

Inside, there was nothing like that.

Once he opened it, Salvi found a piano key that puzzled him. He took it and put it in his pocket, like he had done with the key from the sea.

He continued to explore the tower, and he noticed that, right in the middle of the room next door, there was a piano that was missing precisely the key that he had found. He put the key in its place, and suddenly, the piano started to play itself, to move, and to fly. The floor began to move, and lots of characters came to life, moving to a melody that was somewhere between sweet and disturbing.

While the music became louder, a time custodian, a spinning top, a swan, a flying banana, a snail tamer... and a multitude of other fantastic characters appeared from every corner of the room without rhyme or reason.

The rope skipper, the bread-headed biker, the ants, the winged woman, the stone-man, the penguins with a fried egg, the unicorn... they all started to leave the tower, and to mysteriously follow a long, long path.

That path did not seem to have an end. But it did! That long, black mustache had a destination. It led to a very special drawer. It is where, for a long time, every single fantastic character has been living.

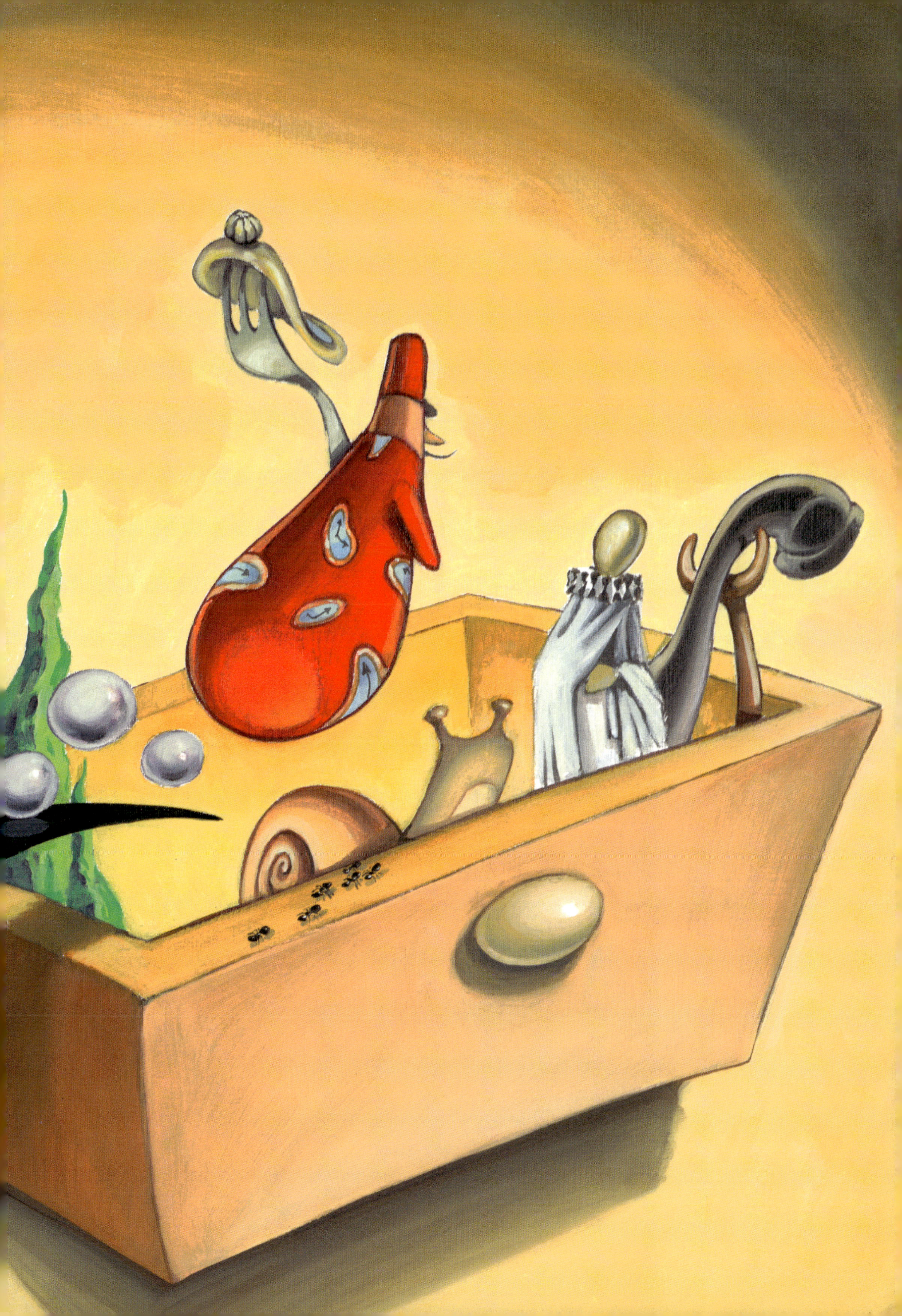

Salvi, like every other child in the world, grew up too. By then, no one called him Salvi anymore; they called him Salvador Dalí. He refused to give up the dreams that his imagination had created during his childhood afternoons. And in order not to forget the world that he himself had made up, he opened the drawer often, and he painted a story for every character. And thanks to that, now everyone knows about his dreams.

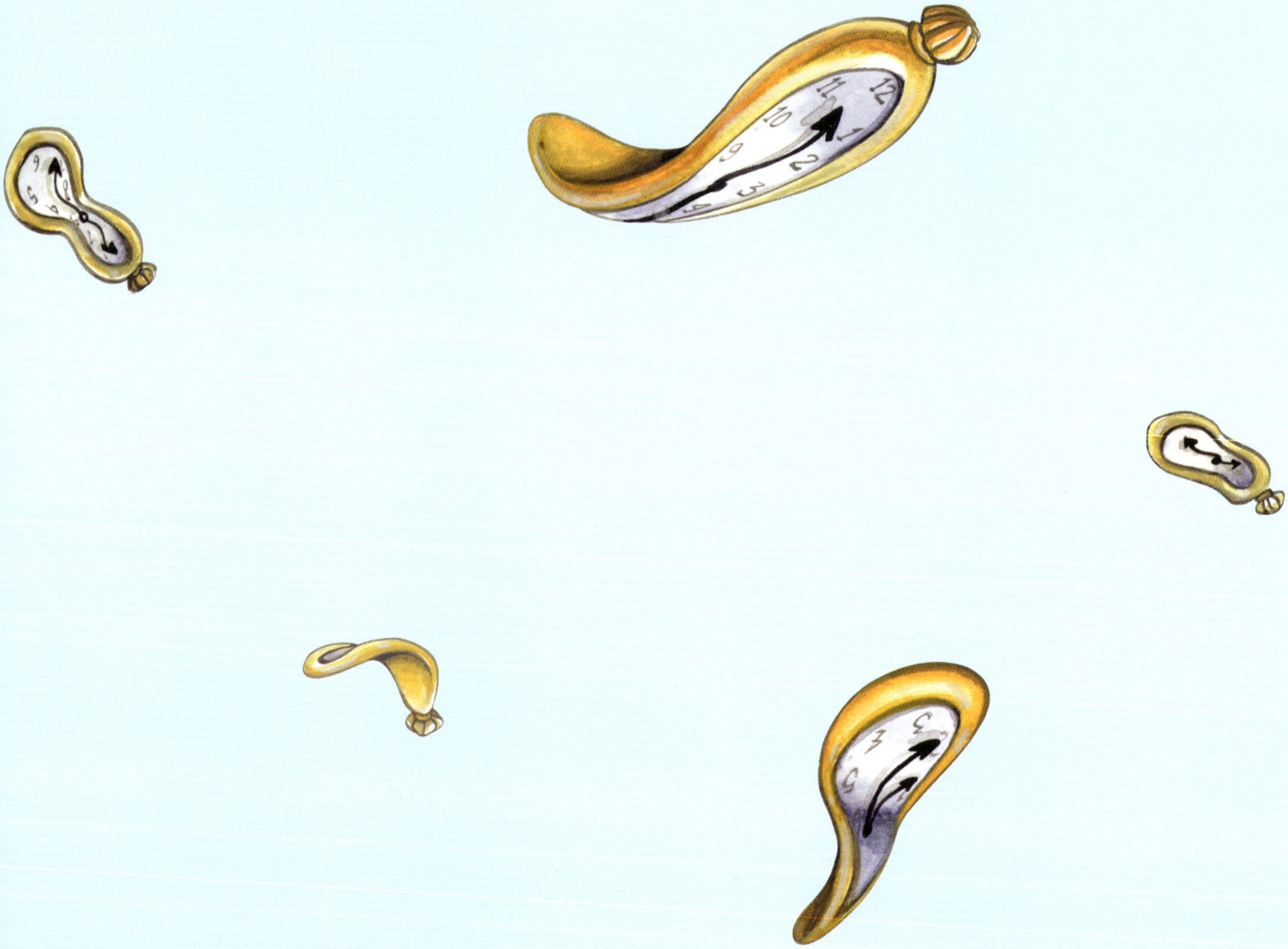

WORKS BY SALVADOR DALÍ

Pages 2-3
Dalí at the Age of Six, When He Thought He Was a Girl, Lifting the Skin of the Water to See a Dog Sleeping in the Shade of the Sea, 1950

Pages 4-5
Project for "As you like it", 1948

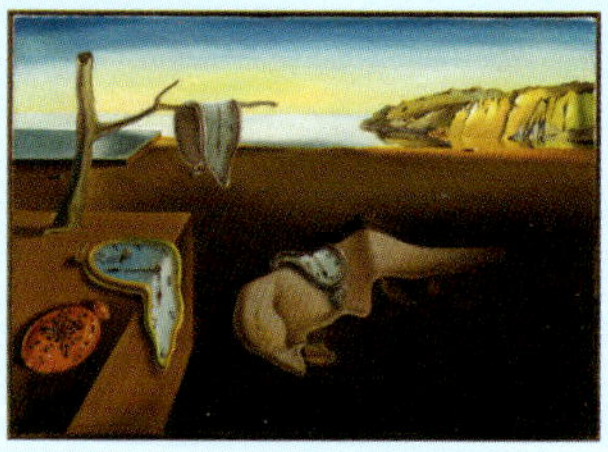

Pages 6-7
The Persistence of Memory, 1931

Page 10
Galatea Tower, 1984

Page 24
Girl at a Window, 1925

Page 24
Atavistic Vestiges after the Rain, 1934

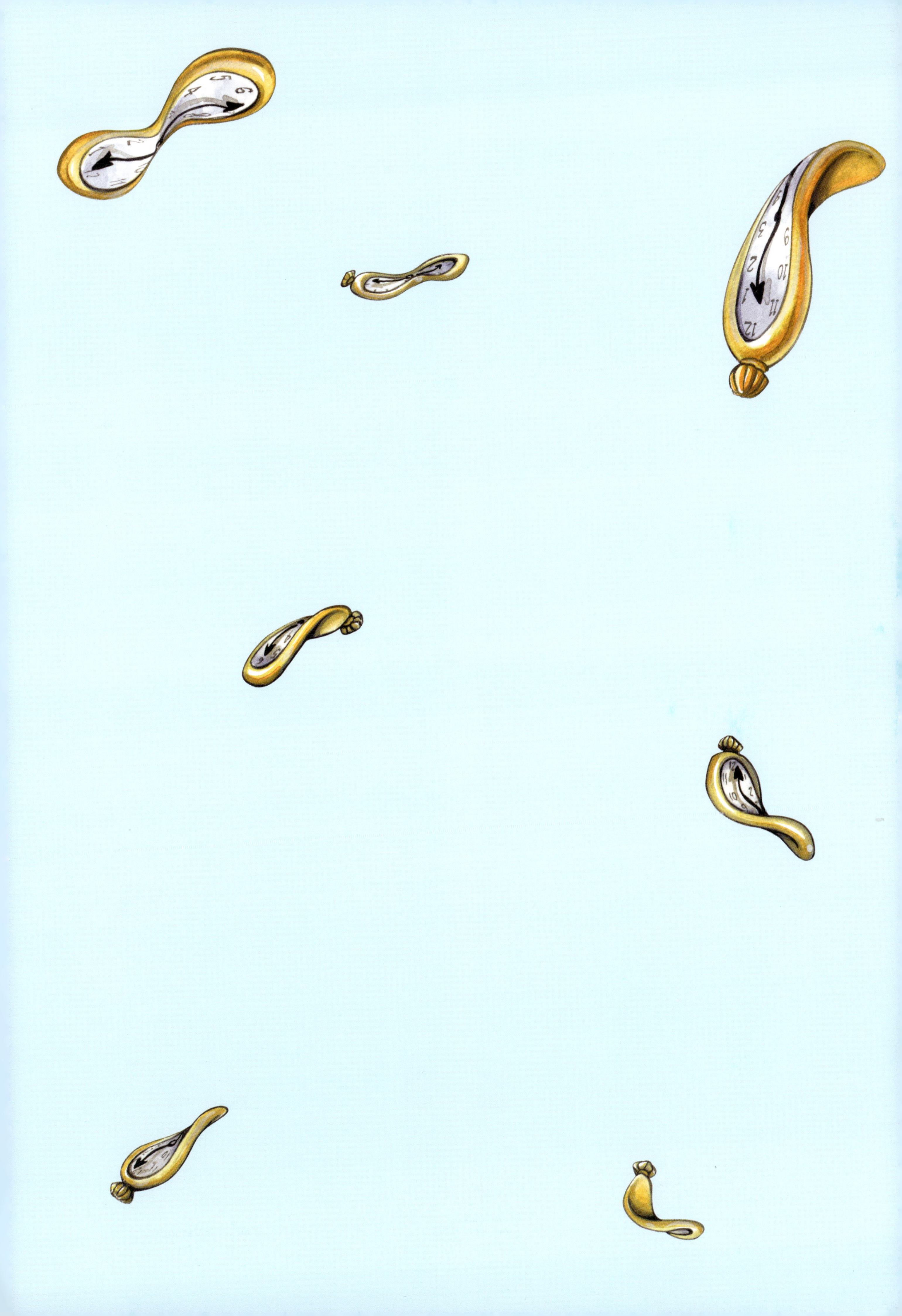